THE CIVIL RIGHTS MARCHES

By Melanie A. Howard

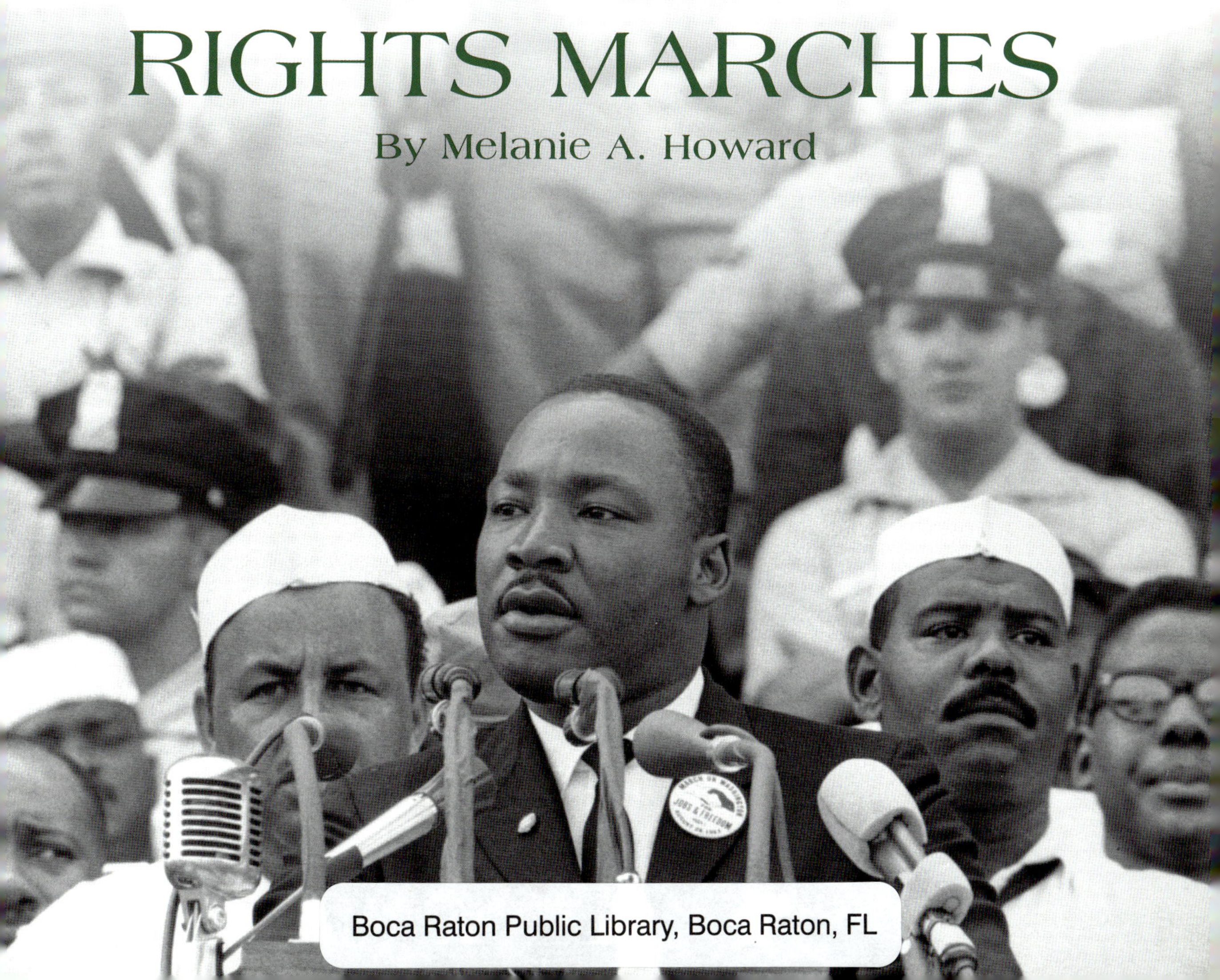

VISIT US AT
WWW.ABDOPUB.COM

Published by ABDO Publishing Company, 4940 Viking Drive, Suite 622, Edina, Minnesota 55435. Copyright ©2004 by Abdo Consulting Group, Inc. International copyrights reserved in all countries. No part of this book may be reproduced in any form without written permission from the publisher.

Printed in the United States.

Edited by: Alan Pierce
Contributing Editor: Katharine Thorbeck
Interior Production and Design: Terry Dunham Incorporated
Cover Design: Mighty Media
Photos: Corbis, Library of Congress

Library of Congress Cataloging-in-Publication Data

Howard, Melanie A.
  The Civil Rights marches / by Melanie A. Howard.
    p. cm.
  Includes index.
  ISBN 1-59197-282-5
  1. African Americans--Civil rights--History--Juvenile literature. 2. Women's rights--United States--History--Juvenile literature. 3. Civil rights movements--United States--History--Juvenile literature. 4. United States--Race relations--Juvenile literature. 5. United States--Social conditions--Juvenile literature. I. Title.

E185.H645 2004
323'.0973--dc22

2003063869

Contents

A Dream of Equality .4
Slavery 6
Jim Crow Laws 12
A Time for Freedom 18
Women Get to Vote 22
Buses and Boycotts 26
Freedom Rides 32
Voting Rights 36
Continuing Fight for Civil Rights 38
Timeline 42
Fast Facts 44
Web Sites 45
Glossary 46
Index 48

A DREAM OF EQUALITY

On August 28, 1963, Dr. Martin Luther King Jr. stood on the steps of the Lincoln Memorial. He stood in front of one of the largest crowds that had ever gathered on the National Mall. More than 250,000 people were packed together on the lawn in a peaceful rally to support African-American voting rights.

African Americans were suffering under the restrictions of unjust laws. By 1963, King had spent eight years fighting for voting rights and an end to segregation. The peaceful protests he had organized were often met with violence. And King had given many electrifying speeches in support of civil rights.

King gave one of his most well-known addresses to the crowd that day. It became known as his "I Have a Dream" speech. The people gathered on the National Mall cheered as King said these words:

I have a dream that one day this nation will rise up and live out the true meaning of its creed: "We hold these truths to be self-evident: that all men are created equal"...

... I have a dream that my four children will one day live in a nation where they will not be judged by the color of their skin but by the content of their character. I have a dream today.

The dream that King spoke of was a goal that many civil rights marchers and protesters have shared. It was a dream that oppressed groups have worked toward for many years. It is a dream that people continue to fight for today. This dream is the dream of equal rights.

Martin Luther King Jr. waves to participants in the March on Washington for Jobs and Freedom on August 28, 1963.

SLAVERY

One group that has fought hard for equal rights is African Americans. This is because they were not officially recognized as citizens before 1865. Before that time, most African Americans were considered property or slaves.

The first slaves were brought to Jamestown, Virginia, in 1619. More than 20 Africans came to Jamestown aboard a Dutch ship. They were traded for supplies.

Virginia and other colonies started drawing up legal documents called slave codes or black codes in the 1660s. Slave codes restricted the rights and freedoms of both free blacks and slaves. Free blacks were told where they were allowed to live, and were given little access to education. Under some colonies' slave codes, free blacks were forced to leave the colony when they gained their freedom.

Slaves fared much worse. The codes stated that slavery was passed down through mothers. This gave slave owners the right to keep any slave woman's child as property. The codes also said that slave marriages were not legal because slaves were not allowed to enter into contracts. Slaves were also not allowed to own property.

At first, most slaves in the colonies were imported from Africa. They were mostly used for agriculture. The slaves planted, harvested, and cultivated crops such as rice, tobacco, and cotton. Some slaves did other tasks such as housekeeping, nursing, trapping, and clearing forests.

Slavery was introduced into the English colonies in 1619 when the crew of a Dutch ship sold more than 20 African slaves to colonists in Jamestown, Virginia.

Gradually, slave owners became less dependent on imported slaves. Because the slave owners were able to keep the children of slaves, the population of slaves born in the colonies continued to increase. This made it less necessary to bring in new slaves from Africa. By the time of the Revolutionary War, only 20 percent of slaves were imported.

In 1783, the Treaty of Paris ended the Revolutionary War and freed the United States from England, but it did not free the slaves. Some authors of the Constitution such as James Madison wanted to end slavery when the United States became a nation. However, slavery continued for almost another 80 years after the ratification of the Bill of Rights.

Slavery was even supported by a compromise made during the Constitutional Convention in 1787. Delegates from southern slave states wanted to include slaves in the census. This arrangement would allow Southern states to have more representatives in Congress.

Northern states did not think it was fair to count slaves as part of the population since slaves couldn't vote. The three-fifths agreement was reached as a compromise. Every five slaves counted as three people.

Many assumed that slavery was going to wither away. Most slaves were kept to farm tobacco, because it was the chief crop in the colonies. But tobacco started to decrease in value by the middle and late 1700s. Some plantation owners began to stop producing tobacco and freed their slaves because the labor was no longer needed.

Then in 1793, Eli Whitney invented the cotton gin. The cotton gin made it possible to clean 50 bales of cotton in a day. Before, one slave could only clean one bale a day. The cotton gin made cotton farming more profitable, and more slaves were needed to support the growing cotton industry.

Slaves working in cotton fields on a plantation in South Carolina

Treatment of slaves varied among plantations and masters. Some slaves, such as George Washington's slaves, were treated very well. Other slaves, however, were treated poorly. Whippings were a common way to keep slaves under control. Slaves who could not be controlled or tried to run away were sometimes killed or sold.

Congress banned the importation of slaves on January 1, 1808. But that did not stop the slave trade in the United States. Slaves could still be sold at any time, and could be forced to leave their families behind.

A number of slaves ran away from their masters. But getting to the free states in the North was sometimes very difficult. Ninety percent of slaves lived in the South where large farms were more

100 DOLLARS REWARD!

Ranaway from the subscriber on the 27th of July, my Black Woman, named

EMILY,

Seventeen years of age, well grown, black color, has a whining voice. She took with her one dark calico and one blue and white dress, a red corded gingham bonnet; a white striped shawl and slippers. I will pay the above reward if taken near the Ohio river on the Kentucky side, or THREE HUNDRED DOLLARS, if taken in the State of Ohio, and delivered to me near Lewisburg, Mason County, Ky.   THO'S. H. WILLIAMS.
August 4, 1853.

A poster announcing a reward for the apprehension and return of a runaway slave named Emily

prevalent. The majority of runaway slaves had to make the journey on foot and without aid. Despite the danger, more than 50,000 slaves had escaped by the 1850s.

Two federal Fugitive Slave Acts were passed to try to stop this, one in 1793 and one in 1850. The Fugitive Slave Act of 1793 gave slave owners the right to pursue slaves who had escaped to the North.

The Fugitive Slave Act of 1850 made it possible for black people who were believed to be slaves to be arrested and given to whoever claimed them. Federal officers also received a fee for returning fugitive slaves. Some federal officers even kidnapped free blacks and sold them to slave owners. The act also imposed a $1,000 fine and six months in prison on anyone who was caught helping a runaway slave.

This did not stop Northern abolitionists from helping slaves escape the South, or keep them from fighting for an end to slavery. Tension between the North and the South over slavery reached a breaking point in the 1860 presidential election.

In the election, Republican presidential candidate Abraham Lincoln defeated Democratic candidate John C. Breckinridge and Constitutional Union candidate John Bell. The South was very alarmed. Lincoln opposed the expansion of slavery to territories and new states, and the South feared that Lincoln would try to end slavery altogether. Eleven Southern states broke away from the Union, triggering the Civil War.

By 1862, President Lincoln and Congress decided to free the slaves in the Confederate states. They hoped to weaken the South by taking away its manpower. But Lincoln's cabinet convinced him to wait to free the slaves until after a Union victory. The cabinet feared that it might seem as though Lincoln freed the slaves out of desperation otherwise.

After an important Union victory at the Battle of Antietam in Maryland, Lincoln issued the Emancipation Proclamation on January 1, 1863. All slaves in the states that had seceded from the Union were declared free. Slaves in states that had not seceded from the Union or that were under Union control were not freed.

Confederate slaves weren't actually freed either, because the states affected by the Emancipation Proclamation were still under Confederate control. But the proclamation affirmed the Union's position on slavery, and set the groundwork for abolishing slavery after the Civil War ended in 1865.

Soon after, Congress passed the Thirteenth Amendment to the Constitution. The Thirteenth Amendment ended slavery. But the African-American struggle for civil rights was just beginning.

JIM CROW LAWS

After the Civil War, there was a period of time called Reconstruction when the Republican Party gained control of the South. Republicans started to break down the oppression that African Americans had been forced to endure. The Fourteenth and Fifteenth Amendments were passed, which guaranteed African Americans citizenship and the right to vote in the United States.

Under the Republicans, the Freedmen's Bureau was established in 1865. This government agency created schools, provided legal aid, and gave out food and medical supplies to African Americans. It also watched over labor relations, and offered African Americans protection from violence. By the time Congress eliminated it in 1872, the bureau had built more than 1,000 schools.

African Americans began to hold political offices during Reconstruction. In 1870, Hiram Revels was elected to the U.S. Senate. Blanche K. Bruce joined him there in 1874. Joseph H. Rainey became the first African American in the U.S. House of Representatives in 1870.

Congress passed the Civil Rights Act of 1875, ending segregation in public places. It seemed that Reconstruction would continue to bring improvements for African Americans.

But then the Democratic Party regained control of the South in 1877. The party established laws that came to be known as Jim Crow. Jim Crow put many restrictions on what African Americans could do

OLIVER OTIS HOWARD

Oliver Otis Howard directed the Freedmen's Bureau from 1865 to 1872. Howard, a Union general, was appointed to the post because of his concern for the newly freed slaves. Under Howard's leadership, the bureau's greatest success was promoting education for African Americans. His work with the bureau led to Howard University in Washington DC being named after him. He served as the university's president from 1869 to 1874.

In 1948, a sign at a Maryland restaurant demonstrates Jim Crow. African Americans must use the rear entrance, while whites can enter through the front door.

and where they could go. Voting, traveling, and getting a job were just a few things that were affected by Jim Crow legislation.

Under Jim Crow, strict laws about segregation began to emerge. In 1881, Tennessee passed a law requiring black and white passengers to ride in separate railway cars. Mississippi, Florida, and Texas passed similar laws during the next eight years.

U.S. Supreme Court decisions of the time helped to keep segregation legal. In 1883, the Supreme Court ruled that Congress had no power to legislate equality. This meant that Congressional acts to protect civil rights were unlawful.

But the Supreme Court went further than that. In 1896, the Supreme Court upheld segregation in the *Plessy v. Ferguson* case.

In many Southern states, African Americans and whites used separate drinking fountains. This form of Jim Crow was one way to limit social contact between blacks and whites.

An African American named Homer Plessy was recruited to ride in a whites-only car in Louisiana and be arrested by the railroad. The railroad hoped that by having the case go to trial, Plessy would win and the railroad would not have to keep separate cars for white and black passengers. Instead, Plessy was thrown in a New Orleans jail.

He appealed to the Louisiana Supreme Court, saying that he should not have been convicted of a crime for what he did. The Louisiana Supreme Court, however, let his conviction stand. So Plessy appealed to the U.S. Supreme Court.

Plessy v. Ferguson was the case of Homer Plessy against Judge John H. Ferguson, the trial judge who had convicted Plessy. In 1896, the

Supreme Court upheld Ferguson's decision. Plessy was forced to pay a fine of $25 or spend 20 days in jail.

Many were shocked by the decision. Supreme Court justice John Marshall Harlan disagreed with the opinion. He said, "The present decision . . . will not only stimulate aggressions, more or less brutal and irritating, upon the admitted rights of colored citizens, but will encourage the belief that it is possible, by means of state enactments, to defeat the beneficent purposes which the people of the United States had in view when they adopted the recent [Thirteenth and Fourteenth] amendments of the Constitution."

He was right. *Plessy v. Ferguson* established the precedent that came to be known as "separate but equal." The precedent meant that segregation was legal as long as facilities for African Americans were equal to facilities for whites.

Jim Crow became even more powerful because of the ruling. Signs that said "for colored people only" or "for whites only" appeared throughout the South. They were posted over drinking fountains, in bus stations, in shop windows, and in restaurants. African Americans and whites even had to go to separate schools.

Even voting rights were affected. Mississippi was the first state to restrict the voting rights of African Americans. By 1910, every state that had been in the Confederacy had voter restrictions like Mississippi's.

African Americans were stopped from voting in several ways. Early on, whites used fraud and violence to keep African Americans from voting. Then they made literacy tests that African Americans had to pass in order to become registered voters. During slavery, it had been illegal to teach slaves how to read. So literacy was low among African Americans after the Civil War.

Poll taxes were another way that African Americans were kept from voting. Usually, African Americans had to settle for low-paying jobs. A tax on voting discouraged African Americans from voting because they could not afford the tax.

African Americans were also kept out of political office. White groups held the primaries for elections, and African Americans were not allowed to participate. The groups justified the primaries legally by saying that the primaries were private clubs, so the government couldn't break them up. People could only vote for the candidates who were chosen in the primary. The primaries became the real election.

Also, African Americans who tried to vote or run for office were lynched. Groups such as the Ku Klux Klan carried out this violence.

KU KLUX KLAN

The Ku Klux Klan was founded between 1865 and 1866 by six soldiers who had been in the Confederate army during the Civil War. This organization worked to protect the idea of "white supremacy." Klan members believed that African Americans were inferior and committed violence against them. Although the Klan was officially disbanded in 1869, the Ku Klux Klan has never completely died out.

Poster for a Ku Klux Klan camp

17

A TIME FOR FREEDOM

Between the 1870s and the 1950s, making a bid for civil rights was not only hard, but also dangerous. But several African-American civil rights groups started up anyway. They bravely spoke out against segregation and made pleas for equal rights.

In 1890, T. Thomas Fortune founded the National Afro-American League. The goals of the league were to stop the disenfranchisement of African Americans and to stop lynchings. Soon after the league was founded, the National Association of Colored Men and the National Association of Colored Women were formed. These led to the creation of the National Afro-American Council.

The National Afro-American Council had several goals. It supported taking legal action against lynching. It also supported higher education for African Americans. This council lasted until 1906. The Niagara Movement adopted many of the council's platforms.

In July 1905, the Niagara Movement was started. Essayist and civil rights activist W. E. B. Du Bois and 28 other African Americans met at Niagara Falls and started a movement that lasted for five years. The Niagara Movement was dedicated to education for African Americans. Desegregation and equal rights were other ideas that the movement promoted. Du Bois openly condemned the violence and oppression white people had inflicted on African Americans.

Booker T. Washington, the most important African-American leader at the time, opposed the Niagara Movement's ideas. He believed that African Americans should learn trades and gradually integrate themselves into society. Washington disrupted the movement's meetings and tried to keep news about it out of the newspapers.

Problems other than Washington's hostility also weakened the movement. The Niagara Movement didn't have the central leadership needed to keep it going. By 1910, the movement had broken down. Du Bois joined the National Association for the Advancement of Colored People (NAACP). He took many of his supporters with him.

Booker T. Washington

The NAACP started after a race riot in Springfield, Illinois, in 1908. Race riots were not uncommon in the South, and there had been a few in the North before this one. But because Springfield was Abraham Lincoln's home for many years, this race riot received a lot of media attention.

Rioting began after a white railroad employee claimed that his wife had been raped by a young African American named George Richardson. Richardson was arrested, and put in jail to wait for his trial. But the sheriff feared that people would try to kill him. So the sheriff decided to move Richardson to another city.

A mob converged on the jail after Richardson was removed. When the members of the mob found out that Richardson was gone, they became very angry. They attacked the restaurant of the man who had given the sheriff an automobile to take Richardson away. Then they set fire to the automobile.

Later, they turned their rage on African-American businesses and homes. Many African Americans fled, but some were caught by the mob. Six African Americans were shot and killed during the riot. Two were hanged. More than 80 people were injured. The tragic event horrified many people. Mary White Ovington decided to take action.

Ovington read about the riot in a newspaper. It convinced her that there needed to be an organization to protect African Americans' rights. She met with the man who had written the article she'd read, William English Walling. Together, with Oswald Garrison Villard, they founded the NAACP.

On February 12, 1909, the NAACP held its first meeting. This was the one hundredth anniversary of Abraham Lincoln's birthday. A later conference in March made the NAACP a permanent organization.

By 1919, the NAACP had 310 branches and more than 91,000 members. It printed a newspaper called *The Crisis* to draw attention to the struggles of African Americans. Soon, the NAACP became a prominent defender of civil rights.

Mary White Ovington

WOMEN GET TO VOTE

While African Americans were struggling for civil rights, women had also begun struggling for the right to vote. Many women believed that having the right to vote made a person a true citizen of the United States. Early women's rights movements focused on gaining the right to vote because of this.

In July 1848, Lucretia Coffin Mott and Elizabeth Cady Stanton called together the first women's rights convention. More than 100 men and women met at a church in Seneca Falls, New York. They drew up a Declaration of Sentiments, and decided that their main goal was going to be getting women the right to vote.

Susan B. Anthony

At first, the women's rights activists wanted to fight for voting rights for all U.S. citizens being deprived of the right to vote. But in 1868, it became clear that some people were willing to settle for giving African Americans and not women the right to vote.

This was not acceptable to several suffragists, and the movement split up into smaller groups. Stanton and Susan B. Anthony created the National Woman Suffrage Association in 1869. This group wanted the federal government to give women the right to vote.

WOMEN'S VOTING RIGHTS IN THE UNITED STATES

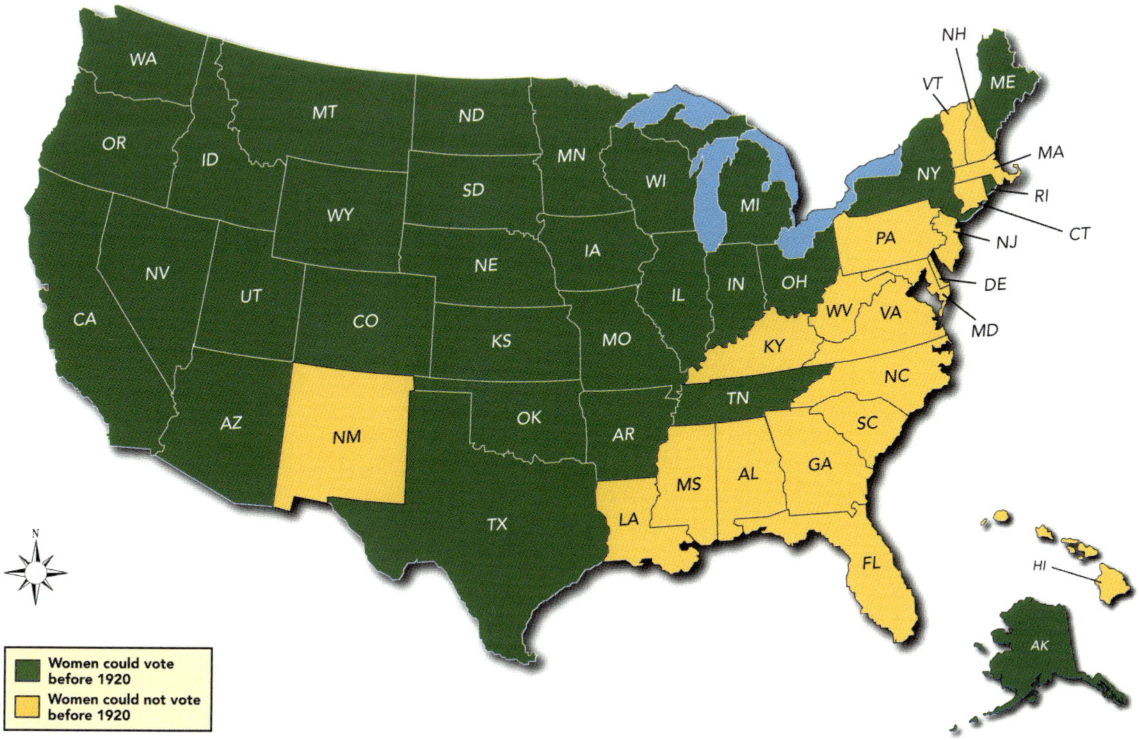

Legend:
- Women could vote before 1920
- Women could not vote before 1920

This map shows which states gave women the right to vote before ratification of the Nineteenth Amendment in 1920. After the Nineteenth Amendment, women were granted full voting rights in all states.

A group of women gathers outside the Woman's Suffrage Headquarters in Cleveland, Ohio, in 1912. They were trying to persuade men to vote for an amendment in favor of suffrage. On September 3 of that year, an election was held to decide whether or not women would be granted the right to vote in Ohio. The amendment failed to pass.

Another group called the American Woman Suffrage Association was founded by Lucy Stone and Henry Ward Beecher that same year. The association did not try to persuade the federal government to give women the right to vote. Instead, it worked for women's voting rights in the states and territories. Suffragists were more successful on this level. Wyoming became the first territory to grant women this right in 1869.

After Susan B. Anthony was arrested for registering to vote in 1890, the two groups came together. They became known as the National American Woman Suffrage Association (NAWSA). NAWSA got Arizona, Washington, Kansas, California, New York, and several other states to give women the right to vote. The association also collected 500,000 signatures on a petition to send to the federal government in support of giving women the right to vote in 1910.

In 1912, former president Theodore Roosevelt ran for president again. He was the Progressive Party's candidate. The party was the first to support women's right to vote. Though Roosevelt did not win, Congress began to look at the issue. Congress then approved the Nineteenth Amendment to the Constitution. It guaranteed women the right to vote. The amendment was ratified in August 1920.

Three years later, a woman who had been a member of NAWSA, Alice Paul, drew up the Equal Rights Amendment (ERA). Paul was the founder of the National Women's Party (NWP). She felt that there needed to be another amendment to the Constitution that would safeguard women's rights. Congress debated the ERA for the first time in the fall of 1923. It was defeated.

Lucretia Coffin Mott

Elizabeth Cady Stanton (left) and Susan B. Anthony

Lucy Stone

Henry Ward Beecher

Theodore Roosevelt

Alice Paul

BUSES AND BOYCOTTS

African Americans were also having difficulty in their fight for equal rights. By the 1950s, Jim Crow laws were still in effect in many states despite the hard work of the NAACP. One of the biggest cases that the NAACP helped push to the higher courts was *Brown v. Board of Education of Topeka*.

Brown v. Board of Education of Topeka was a case about segregation in schools in Kansas. Reverend Oliver Brown's daughter, Linda Brown, was forced to take a bus to a school an hour and twenty minutes away from her home because the nearest school was for whites only.

During the case, Brown's lawyers attacked the *Plessy v. Ferguson* precedent that said that separate could be equal. They provided statistics that showed that the government spent $180 on each white student. The government spent less than $50 per African-American student.

The Supreme Court agreed with Brown's lawyers. On May 17, 1954, the Supreme Court overturned *Plessy v. Ferguson* by saying that segregation in public schools was unequal, and should be abolished. The Supreme Court then started a process that would take many years. It began desegregating schools.

Brown v. Board of Education of Topeka was credited as the case that reversed *Plessy v. Ferguson*. This was also a big victory for the NAACP.

Lawyers for the Brown family congratulate each other after the Supreme Court ruled to end segregation in schools. From the left are George E. C. Hayes, Thurgood Marshall, and James Nabri. Marshall later became the first African-American Supreme Court justice.

But the NAACP's fight was not finished. The NAACP was still opposed to segregation, and was trying to get rid of it in all areas.

For a few years, there had been talk about boycotting the bus system in Montgomery, Alabama. Many African Americans felt that they were not getting fair treatment from the bus company. On the Montgomery buses, African Americans were required to sit in the back. They were also required to give up their seats to white passengers if the bus became full.

On December 1, 1955, Rosa Parks decided to take a bus home from work. The seats on the bus soon filled up, and then another white man got on board. Because she was in the first seat behind the white section of the bus, the bus driver told Parks to move. She was very tired, and refused to give up her seat. The driver had Parks arrested.

Rosa Parks on a bus in Montgomery, Alabama

Parks was not the first African American to refuse to give up a bus seat. But she was a prominent member of the NAACP. Because she was so well known, her arrest made many African Americans angry. African-American activists formed the Montgomery Improvement Association. Members of the association intended to boycott the city buses.

The Montgomery Improvement Association elected Martin Luther King Jr. as its president. King was new to the city, and many thought that it would be better to elect someone who didn't have any enemies. Also, King had been praised for his public speaking while he attended Morehouse College in Atlanta, Georgia. Many who had heard King speak thought that he was the ideal choice.

For 381 days, many African Americans refused to use the bus. They tried hard to find other transportation. This was not always easy. Fewer people owned cars in the 1950s than today. Many of the boycotters walked.

Martin Luther King Jr.

The boycott attracted national attention. In November 1956, a federal court ordered Montgomery to desegregate its buses. Reluctantly, the city did.

King also gained national attention for the first time. In 1957, he and several other ministers founded the Southern Christian Leadership Conference (SCLC). The SCLC wanted to help the NAACP's legal efforts on behalf of African Americans.

On May 17 of that year, the SCLC led the Prayer Pilgrimage to Washington DC. King spoke to a crowd of 15,000 people. He urged the government to help African Americans who wanted to vote. King pointed out that many improper tactics were still preventing African Americans from voting.

After the Prayer Pilgrimage, Congress passed the Civil Rights Act of 1957. This act created a civil rights commission to examine discrimination against African-American voters. The U.S. Commission on Civil Rights soon extended its antidiscrimination investigations to include discrimination based on sex, age, national origin, religion, and disability.

Civil rights activists cheered the passage of the Civil Rights Act of 1957. But the activists also knew that the battle for civil rights was not won. Segregation was still strong throughout the South. Activists decided it was time to focus on desegregation.

By 1958, segregation still existed in many schools despite the Supreme Court's ruling in *Brown v. Board of Education of Topeka*. On October 25, a march for integrated schools was staged in Washington DC. Ten thousand students held a Youth March for Integrated Schools rally. They were led by baseball legend Jackie Robinson, and King's close associate, A. Philip Randolph. King's wife, Coretta Scott King, read a statement from her husband who was unable to attend.

The following year, Randolph led another youth march. This time, there were 26,000 students. They brought a petition with 250,000 signatures urging an end to segregation. Even Martin Luther King Jr. was there and gave his speech himself.

Martin Luther King Jr. and A. Philip Randolph lead
the March on Washington for Jobs and Freedom

DID YOU KNOW?

Did you know that in addition to being a civil rights activist, Jackie Robinson was the first African-American player in Major League baseball? In 1947, Jack "Jackie" Roosevelt Robinson signed with the Brooklyn Dodgers. Robinson had to contend with harassment not only from players on other teams, but also on his own team. Despite this, Robinson was voted Rookie of the Year in 1947 and Most Valuable Player in 1949. Robinson retired from baseball in 1956.

FREEDOM RIDES

Soon, more people became involved in the fight for integration. In February 1960, four African-American students named Ezell Blair Jr., Franklin McCain, Joseph McNeil, and David Richmond sat down at a Woolworth's lunchroom counter in Greensboro, North Carolina. It was a whites-only restaurant. The "Greensboro Four" refused to leave the restaurant until they were served. They remained in the restaurant until it closed at 5 PM. This was the first of many sit-ins that students would stage over the next few years.

In April 1960, King and fellow SCLC organizer Ella Baker supported the creation of the Student Nonviolent Coordination Committee (SNCC). It was founded in Raleigh, North Carolina.

SNCC, besides coordinating sit-ins, also participated in the Freedom Rides. Freedom Rides were set up by the Congress of Racial Equality (CORE) to see if segregation still occurred on interstate buses. In 1960, the Supreme Court had ruled that segregation on those buses and at bus stations was illegal. On May 4, 1961, white and African-American students rode buses together from Washington DC to Jackson, Mississippi.

During the Freedom Rides, white students sat at the back of the bus. African-American riders sat at the front. When the bus made a stop, the white students would go to the colored-only waiting area at

(From left to right) Joseph McNeil, Franklin McCain, David Richmond, and Ezell Blair Jr. sit in protest at a whites-only lunch counter in Greensboro, North Carolina.

the bus stop, and the African-American students would go to the whites-only waiting area.

This enraged some people. In Rock Hill, South Carolina, the riders encountered violence. Twenty people battered the riders until police came to stop them. Later, in Anniston and in Birmingham, and then in Montgomery, Alabama, the riders encountered more aggression. Buses were burned and riders were beaten.

The riders were forced to fly back to New Orleans from Montgomery. With the help of the Nashville Student Movement, SNCC staged another Freedom Ride from Nashville to New Orleans. In Jackson, Mississippi, the riders were arrested. This stopped the Freedom Rides, but proved that segregation was still alive.

To combat this segregation, King and the SCLC decided to put more effort behind civil rights protests in Birmingham, Alabama. In 1963, teenagers and schoolchildren joined the SCLC and many protesters in a march through the city. The schoolchildren and teenagers walked through the streets singing.

Birmingham police commissioner Eugene "Bull" Connor was not happy about this. He sent police officers, attack dogs, and firefighters to stop the protesters. Television footage of young African Americans being sprayed by high-pressure fire hoses horrified many Americans. The fire hoses had enough power to push young children down the street and to strip the bark off of trees.

After the protest, King was arrested and sent to jail. He wrote "Letter from a Birmingham Jail" while he was imprisoned there. In the letter, King defended his commitment to nonviolent, consistent action against injustice. He also talked about giving African Americans the rights they had been denied in the United States for more than 340 years.

U.S. president John F. Kennedy had been very angry with Alabama officials for not protecting the Freedom Riders. Now he was furious. He introduced the Civil Rights Bill of 1963. Kennedy hoped to end segregation, especially in Birmingham, Alabama. The bill, if it passed, would end segregation in public places like theaters, hotels, and restaurants.

In August 1963, another march for civil rights was staged in Washington DC. It was during this march that Martin Luther King Jr. gave his famous "I Have a Dream" speech. There were 250,000 people at the march to show their support for Kennedy's Civil Rights Act.

Unfortunately, Kennedy was assassinated in Dallas, Texas, that November. When Congress passed the Civil Rights Act, it was up to President Lyndon B. Johnson to sign it into law on July 2, 1964.

In 1963, a crowd gathered around the Lincoln Memorial to hear speeches during the March on Washington for Jobs and Freedom.

American Moments

VOTING RIGHTS

After this major victory in the fight for desegregation, King turned his attention to voting rights. He organized a march from Selma, Alabama, to Montgomery, Alabama, in 1965.

Alabama governor George Wallace forbade the march. When the march went forward anyway on March 7, 1965, Wallace sent police to stop the marchers. The police beat the marchers and used tear gas against them. This day became known as Bloody Sunday.

On March 21, 1965, King arranged another march for voting rights. This time, he led the group to Montgomery. Federal troops were sent to protect the marchers when it became clear to President Johnson that Wallace was not going to protect them. The marchers made it to Montgomery on March 25. But Wallace would not speak to them.

This angered Johnson, and on August 4, 1965, he signed the Voting Rights Act. The act made the white primaries and poll taxes illegal.

Martin Luther King Jr. was assassinated on April 4, 1968, in Memphis, Tennessee. He had been standing on a balcony outside his hotel room talking to friends when he was killed by a man named James Earl Ray. People rioted in the streets in more than 100 cities all over the United States in protest.

Opposite page: *Alabama governor George Wallace*

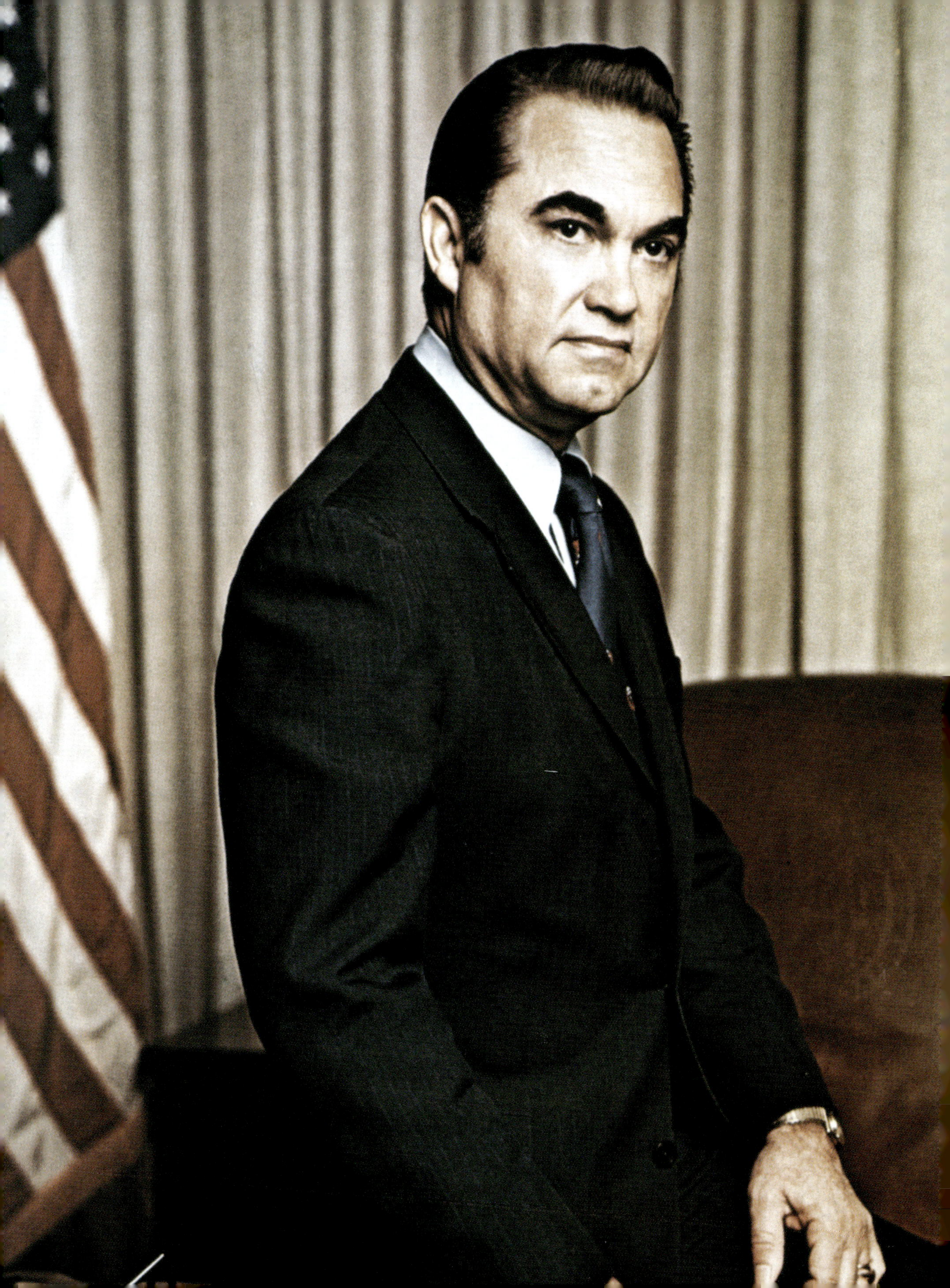

CONTINUING FIGHT FOR CIVIL RIGHTS

The world was saddened by the loss of one of its greatest champions for civil rights. But the fight for civil rights went on. Other groups of people continued to speak out for their rights.

In 1977, the National Women's Party (NWP) and the National Organization for Women (NOW) marched on Washington DC in support of the Equal Rights Amendment. The amendment had been debated since it had been introduced to Congress in 1923.

NOW strongly supported the ERA. The ERA was passed by Congress in 1972, but only 35 of the 38 states needed for ratification supported the law. Because the amendment didn't pass, NOW, NWP, and other women's groups marched on Washington DC.

The women in the march wore white. They decided to reenact a march that Alice Paul had done in the capital in the 1910s. The women wore sashes of purple, white, and gold.

ERA was defeated in Congress in 1983 when it came back up for a vote. Every year after 1985, it has been reintroduced.

In the 2001–2002 meeting of Congress, the ERA was given new hope. It was introduced as Resolution 10 in the Senate, and as Resolution 40 in the House of Representatives without a time limit for ratification. This means that ERA supporters will not have to reintroduce the bill for ratification again.

EQUAL RIGHTS AMENDMENT

- Have ratified the ERA
- Have not ratified the ERA

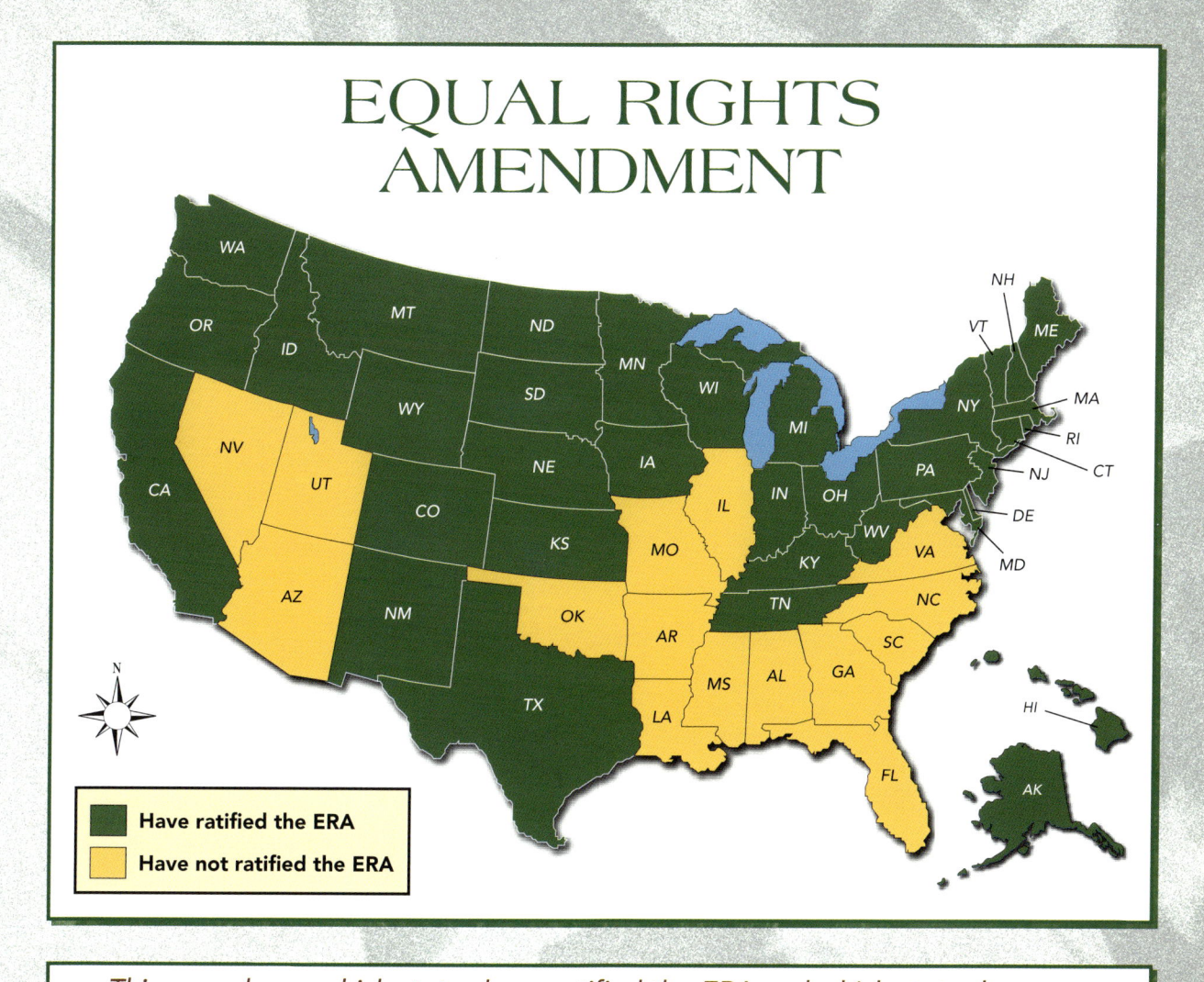

This map shows which states have ratified the ERA and which states have not. Three more states must ratify the ERA for it to become a Constitutional amendment.

In 1976, marchers in Atlanta, Georgia, demonstrated in support of the Equal Rights Amendment. The march took place to commemorate the birthday of Martin Luther King Jr. on January 15.

The Gay, Lesbian, Bisexual, and Transgender (GLBT) community has also fought for civil rights. On April 25, 1993, between 300,000 and 1 million people staged a march on Washington DC for the civil rights of homosexuals.

Marchers asked for the end to segregation in the military and more government funding for AIDS education and treatment. They also asked for civil rights legislation to protect gay, lesbian, bisexual, and transgender people from discrimination. President Bill Clinton was in Boston and unable to attend the march, but he wrote a letter that told the marchers that he supported their concerns.

The GLBT community also held marches in 1979, 1983, and 2000 for their rights. Same-sex marriages are still outlawed in the United States, depriving homosexuals of the right to marry. The protests have covered this issue, as well as discrimination against people with AIDS and support for AIDS treatment.

On August 23, 2003, members of the GLBT community joined thousands of African Americans, Asian Americans, Hispanic Americans, Arab Americans, and whites in a gathering at the Lincoln Memorial. The marchers came to commemorate the day in 1963 that Martin Luther King Jr. gave his "I Have a Dream" speech.

Looking over the diverse members of the crowd, Coretta Scott King spoke these words:

In the four decades that have come and gone since that glorious day of dreams, I have heard my husband's speech quoted more times than I can count. And almost always, they quote from the section of the speech that affirms interracial brotherhood.

Other speakers at the march called for civil rights activists to continue fighting for civil rights, both in the United States and around the world. The march demonstrated that King's dream is still alive. And that there are many who will continue to fight for it.

Martin Luther King Jr. delivers his famous "I Have a Dream" speech to thousands of spectators in Washington DC.

TIMELINE

1865 — Congress passes the Thirteenth Amendment, making slavery illegal.

1920 — The Nineteenth Amendment is ratified, granting women the right to vote.

1923 — The ERA goes to the Congress floor for the first time and is defeated.

1955 — Rosa Parks is arrested on December 1, sparking the Montgomery Bus Boycott, which lasts for 381 days.

1957 — The Southern Christian Leadership Conference is formed. Martin Luther King Jr. gives a speech in Washington DC on May 17 during the Prayer Pilgrimage.

1958 — Jackie Robinson and A. Philip Randolph lead a student march on Washington DC.

1959 — Randolph leads a larger student march on Washington DC.

1963 King gives his famous "I Have a Dream" speech during the March on Washington for Jobs and Freedom on August 28.

1964 President Lyndon B. Johnson signs the Civil Rights Act into law on July 2.

1965 A march on Montgomery, Alabama, for voting rights is staged. President Johnson signs the Voting Rights Act on August 4.

1968 King is assassinated on April 4.

1977 NOW and the NWP march on Washington DC in support of ERA.

1993 Members of the GLBT community march on Washington DC.

2003 Thousands gather at the Lincoln Memorial to commemorate the fortieth anniversary of the March on Washington for Jobs and Freedom.

American Moments

FAST FACTS

Under Jim Crow, Alabama made it illegal for an African-American man and a white man to play checkers together. In Louisiana, it was mandatory for circuses to have a white and an African-American entrance.

Founders of the Niagara Movement were forced to meet on the Canadian side of Niagara Falls. Hotels on the American side of the falls did not allow African Americans to stay there.

The ERA was first introduced to Congress in 1923 by Representative Daniel R. Anthony and Senator Charles Curtis. Anthony was the nephew of Susan B. Anthony, the famous suffragist.

An African-American student named James Meredith tried to enroll in the University of Mississippi in October 1962. Many people were opposed to admitting an African American into the university. This led to violent confrontations, and President John F. Kennedy had to send 3,000 troops and 400 federal marshals to protect Meredith while he enrolled.

Martin Luther King Jr. was a great admirer of the Indian civil rights activist Mohandas Gandhi. King's inspiration for nonviolent protests came from Gandhi's example.

WEB SITES
WWW.ABDOPUB.COM

Would you like to learn more about the Civil Rights Marches? Please visit **www.abdopub.com** to find up-to-date Web site links about the Civil Rights Marches and other American moments. These links are routinely monitored and updated to provide the most current information available.

Martin Luther King Jr. leads hundreds of civil rights demonstrators on the last leg of their Selma to Montgomery 50-mile (80-km) march.

GLOSSARY

abolitionist: someone who is against slavery.

AIDS: Acquired Immunodeficiency Syndrome. AIDS is caused by a virus called Human Immunodeficiency Virus (HIV). The virus attacks white blood cells in the human body, which weakens the immune system. HIV is transmitted through blood or other body fluids and is commonly referred to as a sexually transmitted disease.

Bill of Rights: the first ten amendments to the Constitution. These amendments guarantee most of the state and individual freedoms in the Constitution.

civil rights: the individual rights of a citizen, such as the right to vote or freedom of speech.

civil war: a war between groups in the same country. The United States of America and the Confederate States of America fought a civil war from 1861 to 1865.

Confederate States of America: the country formed by the states of South Carolina, Georgia, Florida, Alabama, Louisiana, Mississippi, Texas, Virginia, Tennessee, Arkansas, and North Carolina that left the Union between 1860 and 1861. It is also called the Confederacy.

Congress: the lawmaking body of the United States. It is made up of the Senate and the House of Representatives. It meets in Washington DC.

constitution: the laws that govern a country.

Constitutional Convention: the convention where the United States Constitution was written.

Constitutional Union: a political party formed on May 9, 1860. The party wanted to find a peaceful solution to the slavery issue. After the 1860 election, the party broke apart, due to the coming of the Civil War.

disenfranchisement: denying a person or people the right to vote.

integration: ending segregation. To desegregate, specifically in schools or other public places that were segregated.

ratify: to officially approve.

Reconstruction: the period of time after the Civil War when laws were passed to help the Southern states rebuild and return to the Union.

Revolutionary War: from 1775 to 1783. A war for independence between England and its North American colonies. The colonists won and created the United States of America.

segregation: to put social or political barriers around certain groups of people based on characteristics such as race, class, or gender.

sit-in: a kind of protest where people sit on chairs or on the floor and refuse to leave.

suffragist: a person who works to gain voting rights. This term is mostly applied to those who supported women's right to vote.

Supreme Court: the highest, most powerful court in the United States.

Union: the states that remained in the United States during the Civil War.

INDEX

A
Anthony, Susan B. 22, 24
B
Baker, Ella 32
Beecher, Henry Ward 24
Bell, John 11
Bill of Rights 8
Bloody Sunday 36
Breckinridge, John C. 11
Brown, Oliver 26
Brown v. Board of Education of Topeka 26, 30
C
Civil Rights Act of 1875 12
Civil Rights Act of 1957 30
Civil Rights Act of 1964 34
Civil War 11, 12, 16
Commission on Civil Rights, U.S. 30
Congress, U.S. 8, 9, 11, 12, 14, 24, 30, 34, 38
Connor, Eugene "Bull" 34
Constitution, U.S. 8, 11, 16, 24
Constitutional Convention 8
Crisis, The 21
D
Democratic Party 11, 12
Du Bois, W. E. B. 18, 19
E
Emancipation Proclamation 11
Equal Rights Amendment (ERA) 24, 38
F
Ferguson, John H. 15, 16
Fifteenth Amendment 12
Fortune, T. Thomas 18
Fourteenth Amendment 12, 16

Freedmen's Bureau 12
Freedom Rides 32–34
Fugitive Slave Acts 10, 11
G
Gay, Lesbian, Bisexual, and Transgender community (GLBT) 40
J
Jim Crow 12, 14, 16, 26
Johnson, Lyndon B. 34, 36
K
Kennedy, John F. 34
King, Coretta Scott 30, 40
King, Martin Luther, Jr. 4, 5, 29, 30, 32, 34, 36, 40, 41
Ku Klux Klan 17
L
Lincoln, Abraham 11, 20
M
Montgomery Bus Boycott 28, 29
Montgomery Improvement Association 28, 29
Mott, Lucretia Coffin 22
N
National Afro-American Council 18
National American Woman Suffrage Association (NAWSA) 24
National Association for the Advancement of Colored People (NAACP) 19–21, 26, 28, 29
National Organization for Women (NOW) 38
National Women's Party (NWP) 24, 38
Niagara Movement 18, 19

Nineteenth Amendment 24
O
Ovington, Mary White 20
P
Parks, Rosa 28
Paul, Alice 24, 38
Plessy, Homer 15, 16
Plessy v. Ferguson 14–16, 26
Prayer Pilgrimage 29, 30
R
Ray, James Earl 36
Reconstruction 12
Republican Party 11, 12
Richardson, George 20
Roosevelt, Theodore 24
S
slave codes 6
Southern Christian Leadership Conference (SCLC) 29, 32, 34
Stanton, Elizabeth Cady 22
Stone, Lucy 24
Student Nonviolent Coordination Committee (SNCC) 32, 33
Supreme Court, U.S. 14–16, 26, 30, 32
T
Thirteenth Amendment 11, 16
V
Villard, Oswald Garrison 20
Voting Rights Act 36
W
Wallace, George 36
Walling, William English 20
Washington, Booker T. 19
Washington DC 29, 30, 32, 34, 38, 40

48

J 323 How
Howard, Melanie A.
The Civil Rights marches /

DISCARDED